Alpha

© Alpha International 2016
First published 1993
Reprinted fifteen times
New revised edition 2014
Updated 2016

10 09 08 07 06 05 04

ISBN: 978 1 909309 73 9

Published by Alpha International, HTB Brompton Road, London SW7 1JA.

Email: internationalpublishing@alpha.org
Website: alpha.org
@alphacourse

Contents

Section 1
Training

Training 1
Small Groups

The aim of this training is to give you all the tools you will need to host or help in an Alpha small group.

The overall purpose of the small group, along with Alpha as a whole, is to help to bring people into a relationship with Jesus Christ by sharing the good news of the gospel (1 Thessalonians 2:2,4,8).

'Alpha is friends bringing friends.'

Nicky Gumbel

1977
Alpha begins at Holy Trinity Brompton (HTB) in London as a course for new Christians

1981
Alpha expands to a 10-week course with a weekend away

1990
Nicky Gumbel takes over the running of Alpha and repositions it for non-churchgoers

1994
Tricia Neill, now President of Alpha, joins the team and rolls out an international strategy

2016
OVER **29,000,000**
people have now tried
Alpha in 169 countries
and 112 languages

2008
10,000,000
people have
experienced
Alpha

1999
1,000,000
people have
experienced
Alpha

1998
OVER **10,000**
churches are
running Alpha

1995
First international
conferences are
held in Africa,
Europe and
North America

Every Alpha session has three key elements:

Food

Talk

Discussion

Guests arrive: welcome them, put them at ease, introduce them to each other. Keep the conversation fun and light and try to avoid talking about deep or heavy topics.

Food: is an important part of Alpha. Eating a simple meal together creates community and helps build friendships.

Worship: this might feel a bit awkward on the first session so it's worth explaining that the guests don't have to join in if they don't want to.

Talk: each session builds on the one before – if guests miss a session, tell them not to worry – they can catch up online at alpha.org.

Discussion: the most important part of Alpha where guests get to say exactly what they think. It's low key, unpressurised and great fun.

Finish on time: have a set finish time and stick to it so guests know when they can leave.

Remember: no pressure, no follow up, no charge.

The perfect size for the small group is

12

Ideally two hosts,
two helpers
and around
eight guests.

11

Three keys to hosting a great Alpha small group

LOVE

Alpha is about sharing God's love through friendship.

'We loved you so much that we were delighted to share with you not only the gospel of God but *our lives as well'* (1 Thessalonians 2:8).

The greatest thing you can do as a host or helper is to share your life with your guests and to love and respect them.

> **'People come to church for a variety of reasons, but they stay for only one – friendship.'**
>
> **John Wimber,**
> Founder of Vineyard Church

LISTEN

Alpha is a chance for the guests to ask anything and say what they think.

The role of the hosts and helpers is to listen; not to have all the answers or to win an argument. Love them, be interested in them and be respectful towards them.

> **'(People) are never so likely to settle a question rightly as when they discuss it freely.'**
>
> ### Thomas Macaulay

The model for the Alpha small group is not teacher-pupil, but host-guest. It is vital to give guests the opportunity to respond to what they have heard and to ask questions in a safe, non-threatening environment.

Groups can be ruined by one of two things:
- Hosts and helpers speaking too much
- Allowing one guest to dominate the discussion

Role of the host:
- Greet newcomers to the group
- Introduce guests to one another
- Facilitate the discussion

Role of the helper:
- Look after the needs of guests
- Handle administration for the group
- Don't say too much in the discussion

Six tips for facilitating a great discussion:

1. **Ask open questions**
2. **Be encouraging**
3. **Be yourself**
4. **Don't answer all of the questions**

Exceptions to asking 'What does anyone else think?'

Questions of fact
Eg, how many Gospels are there?
Eg, where are the toilets?

Direct questions
Eg, why are you a Christian?
Eg, when did it first make sense for you?

Difficult questions
In the first session, make a note of everyone's questions.
If you don't know the answer, tell guests that you'll find
out and get back to them next session.

Recommended reading
Searching Issues by Nicky Gumbel.
Chapters include:
'Why Does God Allow Suffering?'
'What About Other Religions?'
'Is There a Conflict Between Science and Christianity?'
'Is the Trinity Unbiblical, Unbelievable and Irrelevant?'
'What About the New Spirituality?'
'Does Religion Do More Harm Than Good?'
'Is Faith Irrational?'

5. **Don't be afraid of silence**
6. **Rephrase the question**

LAUGH

The experience in the Alpha small group should be low key, relaxed and fun.

Avoid intensity.

In the first session, break the ice with a game and questions to get to know the guests:
1.   Name game
2.   Ask, 'How and why did you end up coming to Alpha?'
3.   Ask, 'If it turned out there was a God after all, and you could ask one question, what would it be?

Remember that laughter is a key component of Alpha.

Have fun and enjoy the journey.

Finally, pray for your Alpha

Prayer undergirds everything we do on Alpha, from beginning to end.

Before you begin
- The pre-session team prayer meetings are vital; a chance to pray for yourself, the team and the guests in your group
- Divide up the group between the hosts and helpers and commit to praying for each guest on a weekly basis

From the front
- In general, we avoid public prayer to avoid guests feeling uncomfortable. However, at the end of session 4 – 'How Can I Have Faith?', there is an opportunity for guests to join in a simple prayer asking Jesus into their life, if they want to
- We don't say 'grace' or pray before the meal

In your small group
- The topic of prayer is introduced in Session 5 – 'Why and How Do I Pray?'
- You may want to offer to say a short closing prayer at the end of the discussion on Session 5 or in any of the subsequent sessions – 'Would anyone mind if I said a short prayer to finish?'
- At some point you may feel it's appropriate to give your guests an opportunity to pray out loud:
  - go around the group and ask each person if there's anything they'd like prayer for
  - a host should start with a very short prayer; long eloquent prayers may be impressive, but they discourage others from praying
  - give space for those who would like to pray, to do so

- one of the helpers should not pray, to avoid putting
  pressure on any guests who may not want to pray
- a host should finish with a short, simple prayer

It is important that the guests have experienced group prayer
before the session 'Does God Heal Today?', where there will be
an opportunity for the guests to pray for one another.

....

....

....

....

....

....

....

....

....

....

....

....

....

....

Training 2
Prayer & The Weekend

The aim of this session is to give you all the tools you'll need to pray with and for the guests on the Alpha Weekend.

The weekend is a crucial part of Alpha:
- Time to get away from the usual routines
- Time to deepen friendships
- Time and space to think and pray
- An opportunity to experience the Holy Spirit

What is prayer ministry?

- Ministry in the broadest sense means 'serving' others
- 'Prayer ministry' means serving others through prayer; 'meeting the needs of others on the basis of God's resources' (John Wimber)
- It is the activity of the Holy Spirit that transforms every aspect of Alpha
- 'Come Holy Spirit' *(Veni Sancte Spiritus)* – the oldest prayer of the church
- We offer ourselves to God as his servants and leave the rest to him

Small Group 1 (Saturday morning):

> 'There are different kinds of gifts, but the
> same Spirit. There are different kinds of
> service, but the same Lord. There are
> different kinds of working, but the same
> God works all of them in everyone. Now
> to each one the manifestation of the
> Spirit is given for the common good.
> To one there is given through the Spirit
> the message of wisdom, to another the
> message of knowledge by means of
> the same Spirit, to another faith by the
> same Spirit, to another gifts of healing
> by that one Spirit, to another miraculous
> powers, to another prophecy, to another
> distinguishing between spirits, to another
> speaking in different kinds of tongues,
> and to still another the interpretation of
> tongues. All these are the work of one
> and the same Spirit, and he gives them to
> each one, just as he determines.'
>
> 1 Corinthians 12:4–11

This discussion is key to facilitating the rest of the weekend:
- Read 1 Corinthians 12:4–11 verse by verse with the group;
  perhaps suggest that each person reads one verse
- Ask guests what they think each of the spiritual gifts
  mentioned might mean

- Make sure you cover, in particular, the gifts of prophecy and speaking in tongues, as these come up in the talk 'How Can I Be Filled with the Holy Spirit?'
- Hosts and helpers should wait until the guests have shared their opinions and experiences before sharing their own

How to pray

1. RESPECT THE INDIVIDUAL

- Sit near your group so that you can easily pray for them
- Offer to pray for each member of your group in turn: men pray with men; women pray with women
- Ask if there is anything specific you can pray for
- They may want to pray a prayer of commitment to Jesus
  - you could use the prayer in the *Why Jesus?* booklet p.18
  - you could use your own prayer: 'sorry,' 'thank you,' 'please'
- They may want to receive a gift of the Spirit
- Confidentiality is important:
  - don't pray loudly, nor gossip with others
  - exceptions: if in doubt, seek the advice of your Alpha Leader or church pastor/priest/minister
- Explain what will happen

2. REMEMBER THE BIBLE

- Pray in line with the word of God: the Spirit of God and the Bible never conflict
- Build on the Bible's promises to encourage and strengthen:
  - freedom from guilt (Romans 8:1)
  - assurances of repentance (Psalm 51)
  - release from fear (Psalm 91)
  - God's guidance (Psalm 37:5)
  - power to overcome temptation (1 Corinthians 10:13)
  - peace in times of anxiety (Philippians 4:6–7)
  - faith in times of doubt (Matthew 7:7–11)

3. RELY ON THE HOLY SPIRIT

'In the same way, the Spirit helps us in our weakness. We do not know what we ought to pray for, but the Spirit himself intercedes for us.' (Romans 8:26)

- Pray simple prayers: 'Come Holy Spirit'; 'Thank you that you love [guest's name]'
- Trust in Jesus' promises: expect the Holy Spirit to come (Luke 11:13)
- Don't be afraid of silence – wait and listen to God
- If you feel God is saying something, ask yourself:
  - is it in line with the Bible
  - is it strengthening, encouraging, comforting?
- Keep your eyes open: watch what is happening
- Avoid intensity: no special 'prayer voice', religious language, eccentricity
- Avoid laying unnecessary burdens on guests, eg lack of faith
- Avoid praying about sensitive subjects: relationships, children, jobs, money
- Avoid criticising other denominations or churches

'… the one who prophesies speaks to people for their strengthening, encouraging and comfort' (1 Corinthians 14:3).

....

....

....

....

....

....

4. RELAX AND TRUST GOD

- Ask: 'What do you sense is happening?' or 'Do you sense God saying something?'
- Refuse to believe that nothing has happened
- Hold on to God's promises (Matthew 7:11)
- Reassure guests that God's promises do not depend on our feelings – some may have physical manifestations, others may feel nothing but God is still at work

Section 2
**Small
Group
Questions**

Hosts' and helpers' preparation

- Each job within the team is vitally important. If you are unable to do the job you've been given, please let the Alpha administrator know
- Please ensure that everyone goes to the team meeting before the session, where important notices and helpful reminders are given

Running order suggestions for a typical Alpha session

- **6.00 pm***
  Prayer and briefing meeting for all hosts and helpers: everyone needs to be clear where their group is sitting for both the meal and discussion time.

- **6.30 pm**
  When the meeting ends, hosts and helpers go to welcome their guests.

- **6.30–7.00 pm**
  As guests arrive, the Alpha administrator should allocate them to a group and introduce them to a runner who will show them to their group.

  One host should stay with the group at all times and the other helpers and hosts can show guests where to pick up their meal. You may have friends who you want to chat to, but remember that your group is your number one priority. You can catch up with your friends another time!

- **7.00 pm**
  Food should be served as quickly as possible to avoid long queues and to allow small groups to talk during the mealtime. Money for the meal can be collected at the serving point (with a sign, 'Suggested Donation').

- **7.28 pm**
  Encourage guests to move their chairs if necessary in order to see the worship leader and speaker.

- **7.30 pm**
  Welcome and notices; book recommendations; introduce speaker; handover to worship leader.

- **7.45 pm**
  Talk starts.

- **8.15 pm**
  Talk ends. Swiftly get into your small group for the discussion time. Delegate the coffee serving to one of the helpers.

- **9.15 pm**
  Make sure you finish on time after each session. As the discussion draws to a close, suggest going on to somewhere (eg café) for a drink together and/or help guests who may be interested in buying books and resources.

You may want to think about how people can purchase books from the recommended reading list, either by directing them online or selling books through your own bookshop.

*Running times have been given as a guide only

Recommended reading

Session 1 – Is there more to life than this?
What's So Amazing About Grace? Philip Yancey

Session 2 – Who is Jesus?
Mere Christianity, C. S. Lewis
Jesus Is, Judah Smith

Session 3 – Why did Jesus die?
The Cross of Christ, John Stott
Searching Issues, Nicky Gumbel
Mud, Sweat and Tears, Bear Grylls

Session 4 – How can I have faith?
The Reason for God, Tim Keller
Life Change, Mark Elsdon-Dew

Session 5 – Why and how do I pray?
Too Busy Not To Pray, Bill Hybels
God on Mute, Pete Greig

Session 6 – Why and how should I read the Bible?
Why Trust the Bible? Amy Orr-Ewing
30 days, Nicky Gumbel
bibleinoneyear.org, Nicky and Pippa Gumbel
Bible in One Year app for iPhone/Android

Session 7 – How does God guide us?
Chasing the Dragon, Jackie Pullinger

Session 8 – How can I resist evil?
Screwtape Letters, C. S. Lewis
Cafe Theology, Mike Lloyd

Session 9 – Why and how should I tell others?
Searching Issues, Nicky Gumbel
Lord... Help Myself Unbelief, John Young

Session 10 – Does God heal today?
Power Evangelism, John Wimber

Session 11 – What about the church?
Questions of Life, Nicky Gumbel

Session 1

Is there more to life than this?

Admin

1. Ensure that you have registered everyone in the group and that each person has a name badge
2. Serve drinks and snacks before beginning the discussion
3. Welcome everyone to the group
4. Introduce yourselves and explain your roles
5. Explain the format for each session and the number of sessions
6. Highlight: no pressure, no follow up, no charge
7. Explain the format and purpose of the small group discussion
8. Reassure the guests that you always finish on time

Icebreakers

These games will enable the group to remember each other's names and get to know one another.

Name Game

- 'Everyone think of a positive adjective that starts with the same letter as your first name' eg 'Jovial John' or 'Happy Helen' OR 'Everyone think of a famous person with the same first name as you' eg 'Justin Bieber', 'Sandra Bullock'

- Start with the person on your left. They must say their name and positive adjective or celebrity name. The next person must say their name and adjective or celebrity name and that of the person before them

- Each person must try and repeat all the names of the guests preceding them from memory. The host is the last person to go and repeats the names of everyone in the group

- Be quick to help any guests who might find this more difficult

Desert Island Game (if you have time)

- 'If you were stuck on a desert island and you could take one thing (not a person) with you, and you already have the Bible and the complete works of Shakespeare, what would you take?'

- OR 'Which person from history would you like to be stuck in a lift with, and why?'

'How and why did you end up coming here today?'

- This gives the rest of the group permission to say what they really think. Try to draw more out of guests if they are a bit hesitant. Start with the guest you think is most reluctant/ hostile about doing Alpha to encourage other guests to open up and be honest

'If it turned out there was a God after all, and you could ask one question, what would it be?'

- Encourage guests, 'These are great questions'
- Write the questions down on a piece of paper with a view to coming back to them at the end of Alpha

Finish on time and carry on discussion elsewhere
(eg, café) for those who want to.

Session 2

Who is Jesus?

Admin

Welcome the group then go around and ask each person to introduce themselves briefly. Welcome any new guests and ask them, 'How and why did you end up coming here today?' Pass around the registration list. Add any new names and contact details and correct any mistakes from the previous session.

Questions for discussion

1. What makes you happy?

2. What do you think about Jesus?

3. If you had a chance to meet Jesus, how would you feel and what would you say to him?

Additional questions (if needed):

4. Before you heard the talk tonight, what was your concept of Jesus? Has it changed? If so, in what way?

5. What aspects of the evidence presented tonight did you find convincing/not convincing?

Textual criticism -
the timelines e.g.
Plato/Bible etc.

Session 3

Why did Jesus die?

Admin

Introduce any new guests. Pass around the registration list. Add any new names and contact details and correct any mistakes from the previous session.

Questions for discussion

This is often the session when the subject of 'suffering' arises (see *Searching Issues* chapter 'Why Does God Allow Suffering?').

1. What does the word 'forgiveness' mean to you?

2. Have you ever had to forgive anyone? How did you do it?

3. What does the word 'sin' mean to you?

Additional question (if needed):

4. What is your reaction to Jesus' death?

Notes   something good that
            happened this week.

"You are loved"
All have sinned and fallen short
Romans 2.1 - you have no
reason to pass judgement.
Sin creates a barrier between
us + god.

- Like someone living rent-free
  in your head

- Drinking poison expecting the
  other person to die

If god forgives you must
forgive yourself

A choice.

do you think marrying on is
  the same as forgiveness

Session 4

How can I have faith?

Admin

Introduce any new guests. Pass around the registration list and amend if needed. This is a good time to mention the Alpha Weekend for the first time. Give the dates to the guests.

Questions for discussion

You may find that guests have questions, for example, about other religions (see *Searching Issues* chapter 'What About Other Religions?').

1. What does faith mean to you?

2. What do you think about the evidence for Christianity?

3. How can you have faith in someone you can't see?

Paul - new creation.

faith - Confidence it pe all

seeing what believing

John 12:2.

Yet to all who received him

Lover + a friend. Husband + a wife

1 John 5:13.

Faith comes from hearing, and

hearing through the word of god.

Romans

Revelation 3..20 - Here I am -

I stand at the door + knock.

If anyone hears my voice. and open

the door, I will come.

Holman Hunt - the light of the

world.

The handle is on the inside.

Putting our trust in Jesus = faith

Prayer @ end.

Remember Jesus you died for us

on the cross.

Session 5

Why and how do I pray?

Admin

This is a good time to encourage guests to attend the Alpha Weekend. Mention the cost and the possibility of bursaries.

Questions for discussion

1. Have you ever tried praying? How did you get on?

2. What do you think about the idea of God answering prayer?

3. Finish with a short prayer (if appropriate)

Additional question (if needed):

4. In the talk, various reasons for praying are given. Which of these do you relate to and why?

"go into your room".

Rewards of prayer?

○ presence of God.

Romans 8. 26

spirit interceds for us.

Does God always answer prayer?

○ a loving parent won't always say yes to requests

Is there anything you've been desperate to do + prayed + it didn't happen?

prayer is about a relationship with God.

Session 6

Why and how should I read the Bible?

Admin

Remind the group about the Alpha Weekend. Ask someone who has benefited from a previous one to describe their experience. Take further names and collect payment.

Questions for discussion

1. Has anyone ever tried reading any of the Bible? How did you find it?

2. How do you feel about the idea of God speaking through the Bible?

3. Has anyone got any practical suggestions about how to read the Bible? (at an appropriate point in discussion, you might recommend the Bible in One Year app: bibleinoneyear.org)

Additional question (if needed):

4. Have you read anything in the Bible that has challenged an aspect of your beliefs or behaviour?

....

....

....

....

....

....

....

....

....

....

....

....

....

....

....

....

....

....

....

Session 7

How does God guide us?

Admin

Arrange transport for the Alpha Weekend if necessary.

Questions for discussion

1. Over the last few weeks, has anyone had a sense that God might be guiding them?

2. How do you feel about the idea of God having a plan for your life?

Peace
Common sense
circumstantial rights

Proverbs 16:9 — The Lord
determines your steps.

Session 8

Who is the Holy Spirit?

There is no small group discussion following this session.

John 15.26 "When the
Counsellor comes, whom I
will send to you from the
Father, the Spirit of Truth
who goes out from the
Father, he will testify about
me."

- H.S makes Jesus real to us.
- sons & daughters.
- The experience of the HS
is a crucial part of the NT.
Come H.S.
Pray a prayer of repentance
first

Receive the gift of enjoying in
tongues / tongues
Bringing people's requests to God
meeting the needs of others on
the basis of God's resources

- Ask if they want prayer
- anything specific
- lead in prayer - sorry, thank you
- re-assure God knows/cares

Romans 8:1 - no condemnation
listening to people's experience
where they will be with God in
10 mins time

Session 9

What does the Holy Spirit do?

Questions for discussion

Read 1 Corinthians 12:4–11.

1. What do you think each of the spiritual gifts refers to? (vv.8–10)

2. What is the gift of tongues? Does anyone have any experience of it?

3. How do you feel about the idea of God giving us supernatural gifts?

4. Does everybody have the same gifts? (vv.4–6)
   • different gifts, works and service, but the same God

5. Why does God give spiritual gifts to people? (v.7)
   • for the common good
   • not for our own glory

6. Mention that there will be an opportunity to hear more on this subject in the next session.

wisdom, knowledge
faith, healing,
powers, prophecy
distinguishing between spirits
tongues
interpretation of tongues.
Tongues is often the first of the
more supernatural gifts.
Sometimes we have a strange
sense of the H.S.
"Be filled with the H.S." – Ongo
on being filled!

Session 10

How can I be filled with the Holy Spirit?

This session is followed by a time of prayer ministry in a corporate setting. Spend time praying with any guests who would like prayer to be filled with the Holy Spirit (see Training 2).

Session 11

How can I make the most of the rest of my life?

Ask each member of the group, starting with the person who will be most open, to describe their experience of the weekend. This will give permission for any others who want to, to share their experiences. If appropriate you may wish to offer an opportunity for the group to pray for one another.

Session 12

How can I resist evil?

Admin

Start the small group time by asking guests to share their experiences of the Alpha Weekend. (Start with the person who will be most open/positive.) This gives the guests the opportunity to express what happened to them. It can be a great encouragement to the group. Remember to include those who did not go on the weekend in the discussion by asking them what they think about what they have heard.

Questions for discussion

1. Feedback from the weekend (see notes above)

2. Why do you think bad things happen?

3. Where does temptation come from?

4. How do you resist temptation?

• logical to believe in the power
of good if there is a power of
evil

                    doubt and doubt
                         and

God wants us to believe or belief
    Devil wants us to doubt or belief
        + belief or doubts

love is always a doubt but it
    requires faith

temptation ~~off~~ often starts
        with doubts.
"Did God really say?"
"If you are the son of God"

kingdom of God has a now
    aspect and a not yet.

kingdom of darkness to the
kingdom of light.

Paul Venice
Steve Tayler.

57

Session 13

How and why should I tell others?

Admin

If you are holding an Alpha celebration evening to mark the end of the course, this is a good time to remind guests of the date and times. Invitations can be handed out too. If possible, aim to pray together as a group at the end of this session.

Questions for discussion

1. Have you told any of your friends/family/colleagues at work that you are doing Alpha? What was their reaction?

2. If you did not know anything about Christianity, how would you like to be told about it?

3. What do you think/feel about the idea of telling others about your faith?

Session 14

Does God heal today?

Admin

Remind guests about the Alpha celebration if you are planning one. Try to work out approximately how many people will be coming, including small group members and any guests they plan to invite.

Prayer for healing

- If words of knowledge were given at the end of the talk, ask if anyone in the group thinks that a 'word of knowledge' may have been for them

- If not, ask your guests if there is a specific problem or illness for which they would like prayer for healing. At the same time ask if anyone would like prayer for any other issue. This is a good time to clear up any general issues about the subject of healing, so allow time for the group to discuss briefly before praying together

- Pray for guests according to the prayer ministry guidelines (Training 2). If there are lots of guests, divide into one group of men and one group of women

- Be prepared for someone who may want to give their life to Christ. Equally affirm those who do want to be prayed for and those who do not

Session 15

What about the church?

Admin

Remind the group about the Alpha celebration or provide details about church on Sunday. Make a date for a small group reunion. This could possibly be at the host's home, ideally about two weeks before the next Alpha starts, or sooner if appropriate.

Ask the guests to complete the Alpha questionnaire to feed back on their experience.

Questions for discussion

1. Go around the group asking each person to summarise what they have learnt and experienced on Alpha. (Try to start with the most open/positive person)

2. Ask the group what they would like to do after Alpha. Try to encourage them to stay connected as a group

3. Ask each of them if there is anything they would like prayer for

4. Pray – it's a good idea to finish the final session with prayer

Optional questions for further discussion

1. What comes to mind when you hear the words 'church' or 'Christian'?

2. Think back to the start of Alpha. Has your view changed?

3. Looking forwards, in what way (if any) do you plan to continue what you've started on Alpha?

Theresa & Steve - gay, drago.
(wheat free)

Cath Renny.
Nat + Kristy
5 from Carnforth
Heather Centre - Lenny's
Steve + Lou.
James Wett (wife @ teacher @
              school)